collective order | marius born | コレクティブ・オーダー

collective order | marius born | コレクティブ・オーダー

Notes on Tokyo

collective: ***1:** denoting a number of persons or things considered as one group or whole <flock is a collective word> | **2:** formed by collecting : aggregated | **3:** involving all members of a group as distinct from its individuals <a collective action> | **4:** marked by similarity among or with the members of a group | **5:** collectivized or characterized by collectivism | 6: shared or assumed by all members of the group <collective responsibility>*

order: *1: a group of people united in a formal way as a fraternal society <the Masonic Order> | **2:** a rank, class, or special group in a community or society | **3:** the arrangement or sequence of objects or of events in time <the batting order> or a sequential arrangement of mathematical elements | **4:** a sociopolitical system <was opposed to changes in the established order> or a particular sphere or aspect of a sociopolitical system <the present economic order> | **5:** a regular or harmonious arrangement <the order of nature> | **6:** the customary mode of procedure especially in debate <point of order> | **7:** the state of peace, freedom from confused or unruly behavior, and respect for law or proper authority <promised to restore law and order> | **8:** a specific rule, regulation, or authoritative direction : command | **9:** a proper, orderly, or functioning condition <their passports were in order> <the phone is out of order> | **10:** a written direction to pay money to someone | **11:** an assigned or requested undertaking <landing men on the moon was a tall order> | **12:** order of the day <flat roofs were the order in the small villages>*

The pictures in "collective order" enable us to take part in Marius Born's impressions of Tokyo and its surroundings. Many occurrences in everyday Japanese life are unaccustomedly different for the Swiss photographer; in the Japanese metropolis he comes up against an order system that he is not familiar with and that he, therefore, wants to capture with his camera. As a result, two cultures, one depicted and one depicting, are interwoven in this book to create a view of a collective (literally, 'put together') order.

The photographer succeeds in capturing in his pictures that even in the urban, densely populated metropolis of Tokyo, the individual occasionally manages to open up some space. Thus, the nocturnal route in the subway passages through which the masses of commuters stream during the day becomes a lonely walk, and cycling in the park of the Emperor, far away from the crowded roads, looks like a ride in the countryside.

At the same time, the individual is always part of the collective, whose forms of order also characterize Japanese everyday life. On the sports ground, for example, girls and boys are ordered by the color of their hats, and the exercises are done in rank and file. For the group photo too, everything is organized: the benches for the photo shoot are installed and the group number on the memorable picture confirms that one is part of a greater order.

The depicted and the depicting oppose each other. This applies to all the photographs in this book. It is especially evident in the pictures of the Japanese taking photographs: Marius Born places himself in the row of his subjects – and, in so doing, becomes part of the collective order himself.

Marlies Whitehouse and Daniel Perrin, Summer 2011

コレクティブ・オ−ダ−の写真は、見る人をマリウス・ボーヌが受けた東京とその近郊の印象の中へと引き入れます。日本で日常生活なものの多くは、スイスの写真家には見慣れぬ未知のものです。日本の大都会で、マリウス・ボ−ヌは未知の秩序のシステムを見て、だからこそそれを写真に収めておきたかったのです。それによって、この本では、写し取られた文化とそれを写し取る文化とが、コレクティブな、つまりひとつに合わされた秩序という視点へと、組み合わされていきます。

人口密度が高い都会の東京で、それぞれが自分の場所を見つけるのを、マリウス・ボ−ヌはいろんな写真で見せてくれます。例えば、昼間はサラリーマンの群れが行き交う地下鉄の通路を歩けば、夜には孤独な散歩になります。そして、交通渋滞から遠く離れて皇居の公園で自転車に乗れば、遠足の気分へとなります。

同時に、それぞれはつねにコレクティブの一部分であり、そのコレクティブな秩序が、日本の日常生活を形作っているのです。たとえば、体育の授業で女の子と男の子は帽子の色でもう一度区別して分けられ、みんな整列して運動しています。皇居の前での集合写真も、しっかり組織されています。写真専用のベンチが用意されていて、記念写真のグループ番号は、一人一人がより大きな秩序の一部分であることを証明しています。

写し取られたものと写し取るものは、お互いに対位しており、これはコレクティブ・オ−ダ−のすべての写真に当てはまります。写真を取っている日本人の写真の中に、それがよく表れています。日本人が写真を取る時、マリウス・ボ−ヌはその題材の側に立っていて、自分自身が、コレクティブな秩序の一部分になるのです。

北口雄一、マリス・ウアイトハウス、ダニエ−ル・ペ−レ−　夏 2011

collective order | marius born

Tameike-Sanno Subway Station, Tokyo, February 15, 1.30am

collective order | marius born

| 10

Shimbashi Subway Station, Tokyo, February 27, 9am

collective order | marius born

| 12

Imperial Palace Plaza, Tokyo, February 26, 10am

collective order | marius born

|14

Imperial Gardens, Tokyo, March 3, 3.30pm

collective order | marius born

| 16

Higashi-Nakano, Tokyo, March 3, 5pm

collective order | marius born

Sogo Sports Park near Tokyo, March 2, 2pm

collective order | marius born

| 20

Sogo Sports Park near Tokyo, March 2, 2pm

collective order | marius born

| 22

Akasaka, Tokyo, March 3, noon

Akasaka, Tokyo, March 3, noon

collective order | marius born

| 26

Gardens of Hama-Rikyu, Tokyo, March 9, 11am

collective order | marius born

| 28

Gardens of Hama-Rikyu, Tokyo, March 1, 11am

collective order | marius born

| 30

Gardens of Hama-Rikyu, Tokyo, July 17, 5pm

collective order | marius born

| 32

Gardens of Hama-Rikyu, Tokyo, July 17, 5pm

collective order | marius born

| 34

Imperial Palace Plaza, Tokyo, March 8, 10am

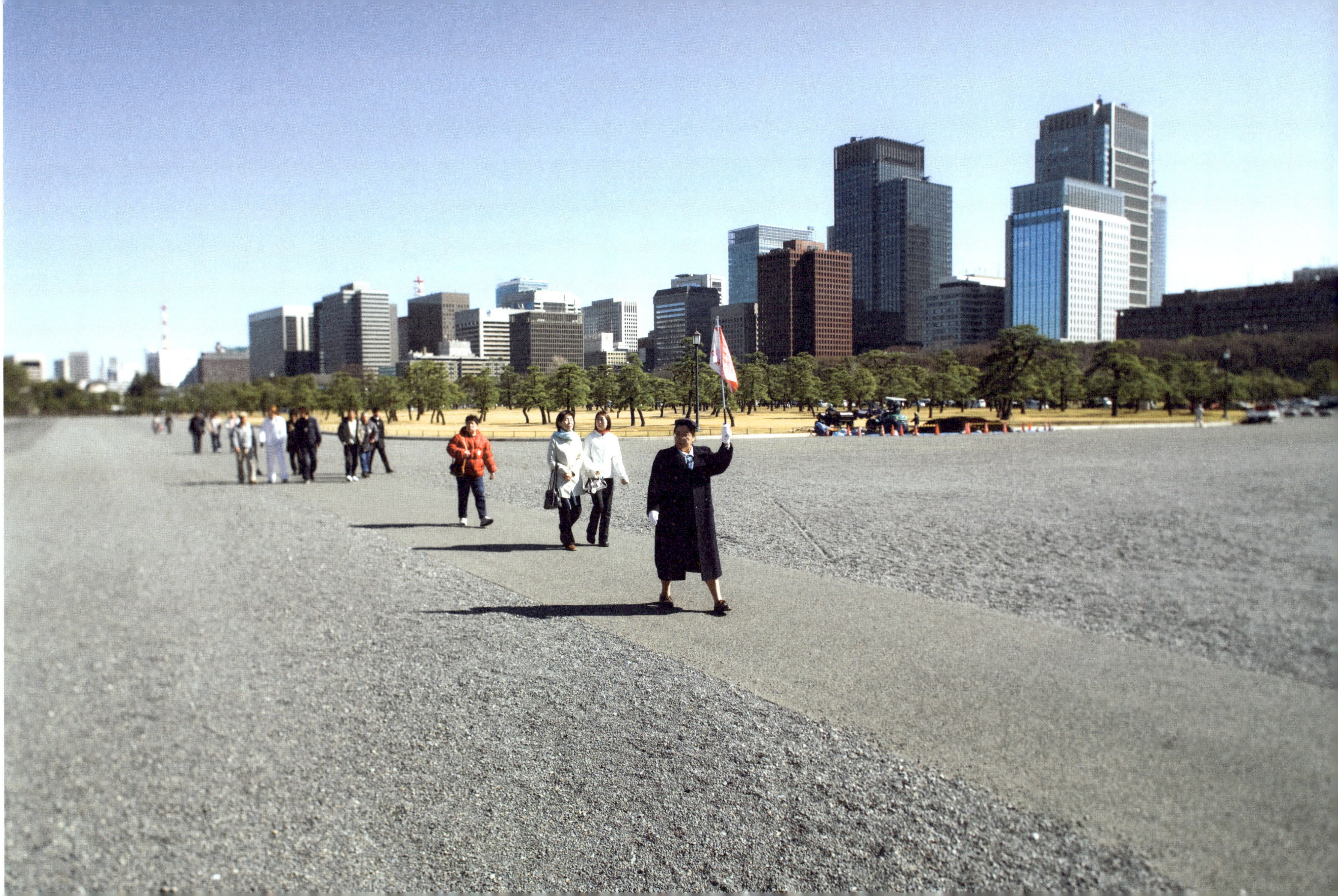

collective order | marius born

| 36

Imperial Palace Plaza, Tokyo, March 3, 2pm

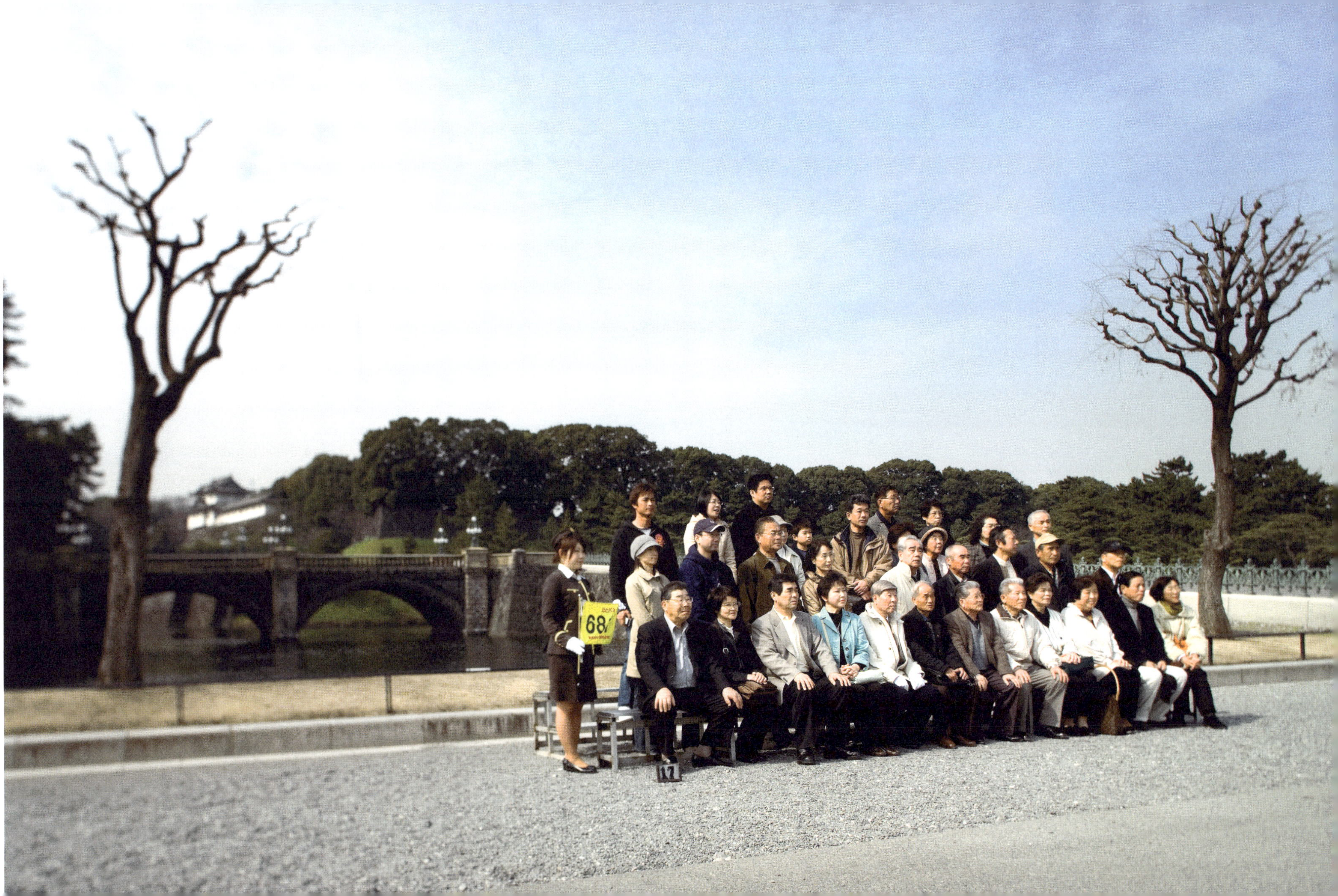
68
17

collective order | marius born

| 38

Tsukiji Fish Market, Tokyo, February 21, 5.30am

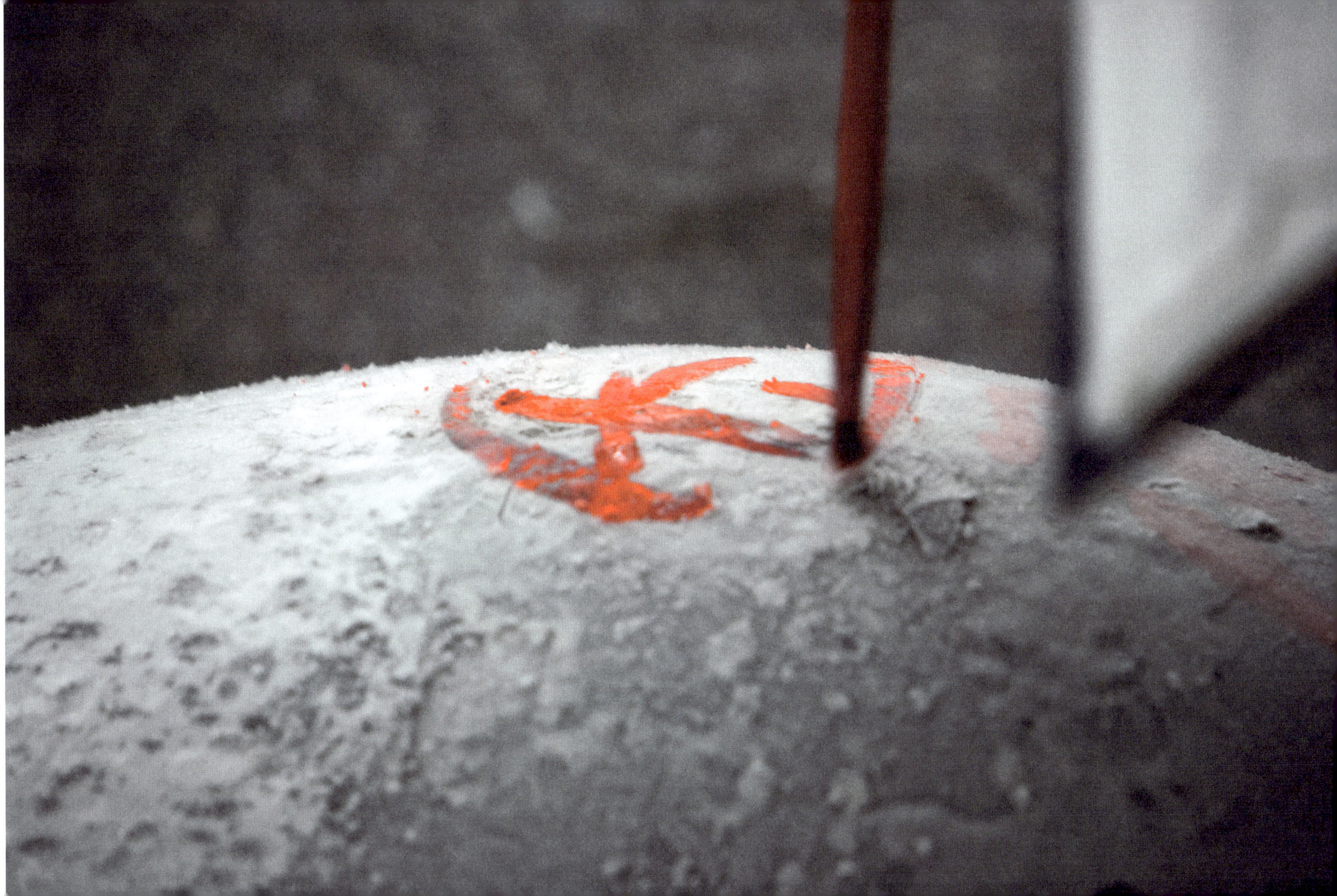

collective order | marius born

Tsukiji Fish Market, Tokyo, February 21, 4.30am

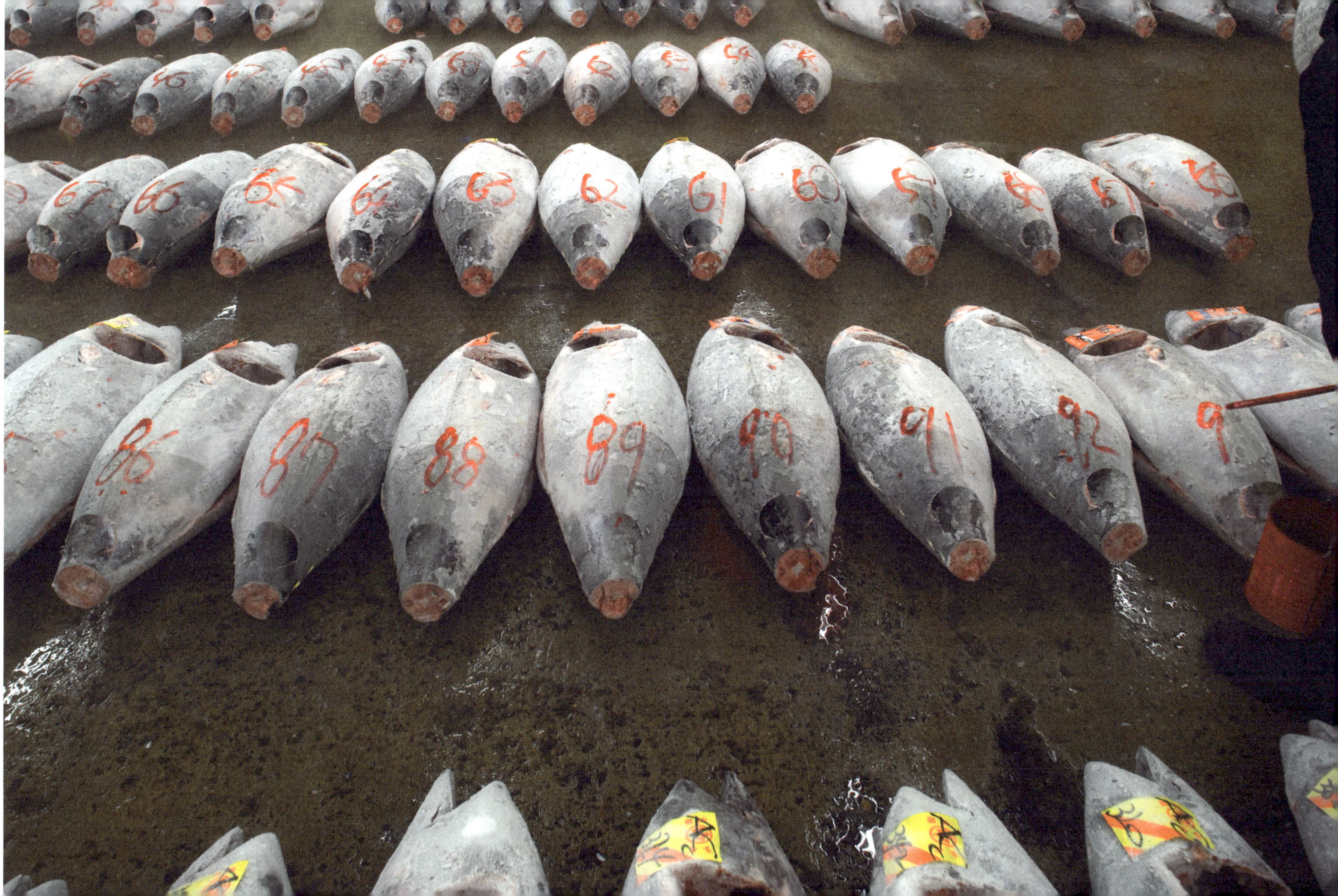
66
63
62
61
86
87
88
89
90
91
92

collective order | marius born

| 42

Tsukiji Fish Market, Tokyo, February 22, 8am

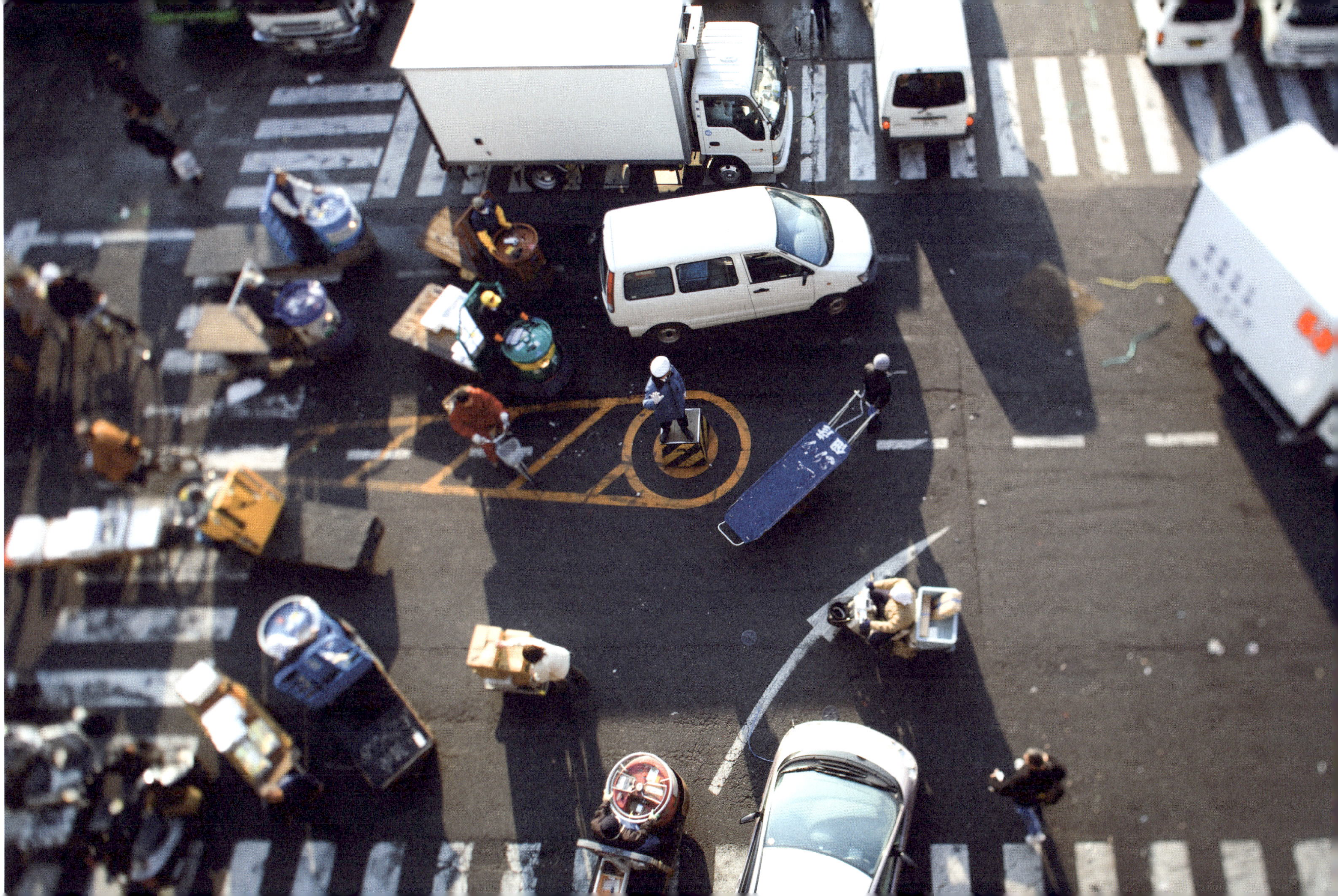

collective order | marius born

| 44

Tsukiji Fish Market, Tokyo, February 21, 5am

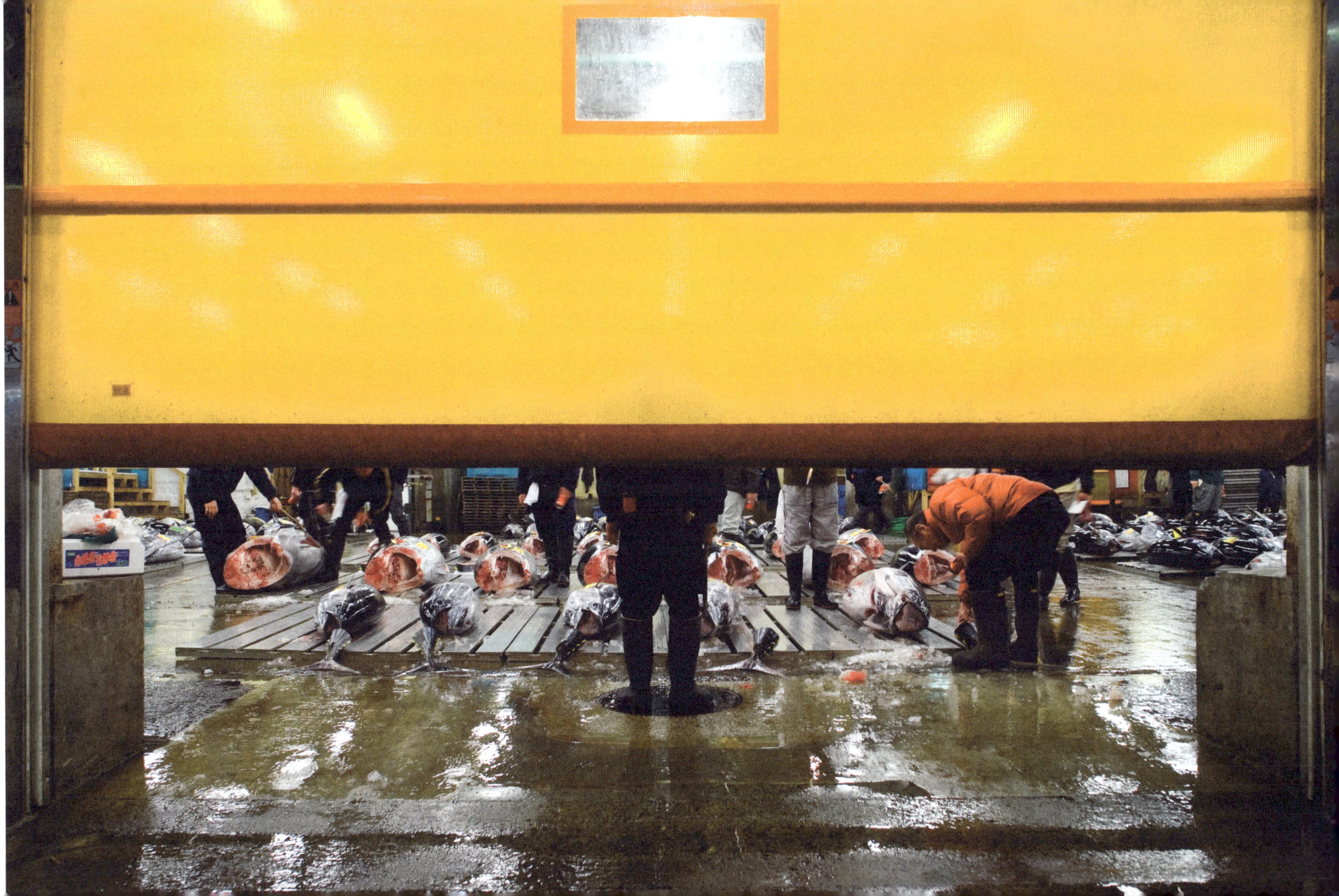

collective order | marius born

| 46

Tameike-Sanno Subway Station, Tokyo, February 21, 7pm

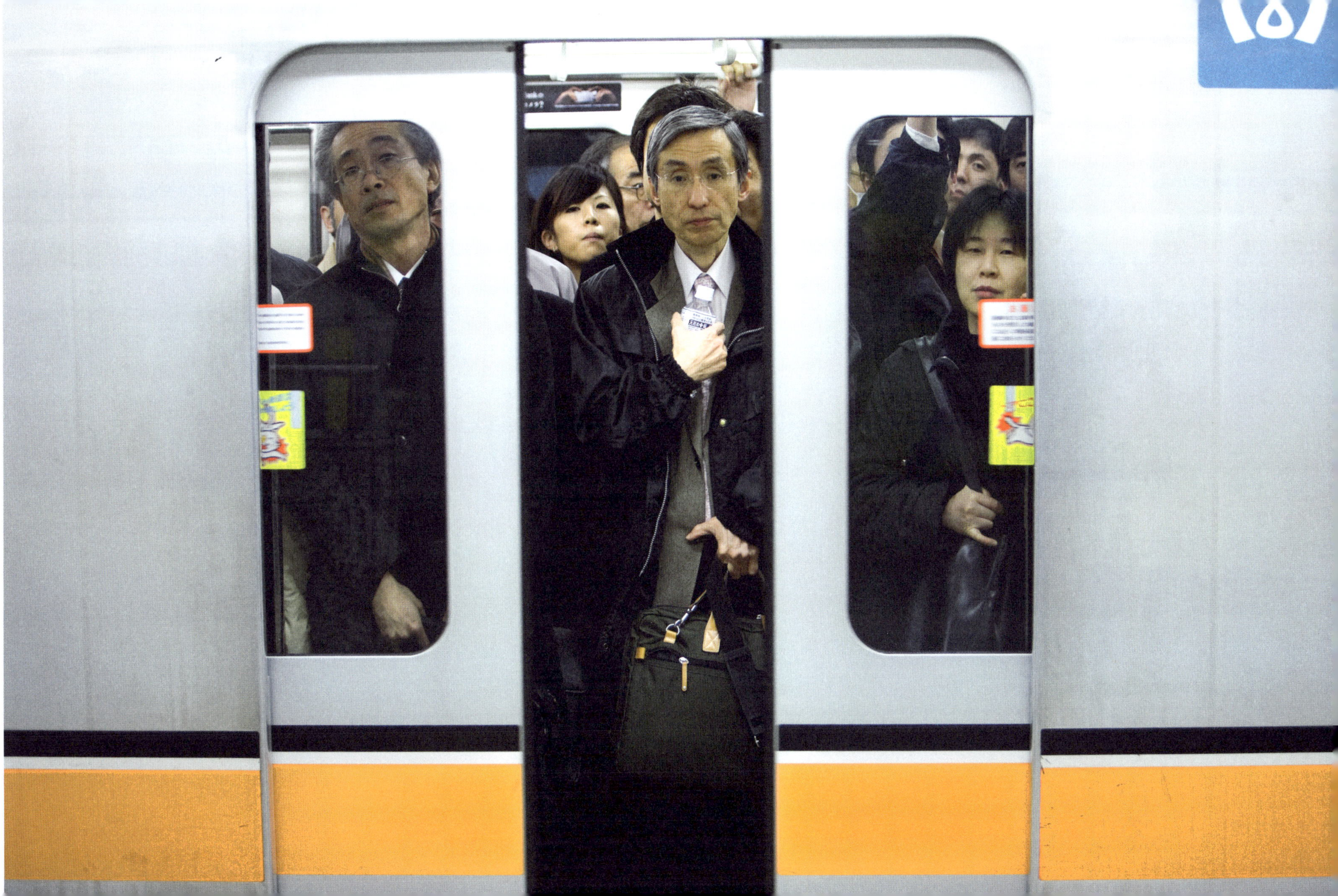

collective order | marius born

| 48

Fujikyu Highland near Tokyo, February 25, noon

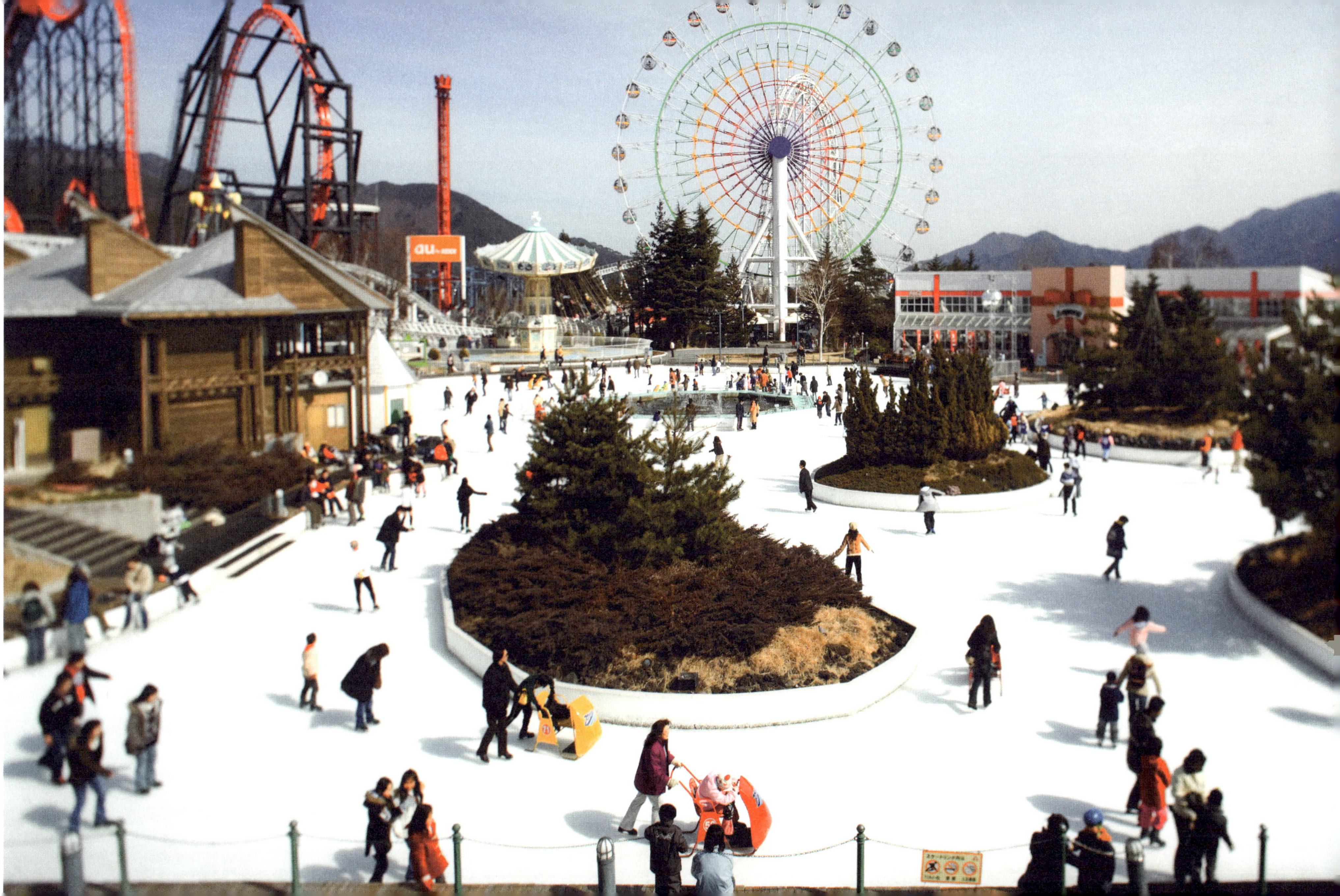
au

collective order | marius born

| 50

Fujikyu Highland near Tokyo, February 25, noon

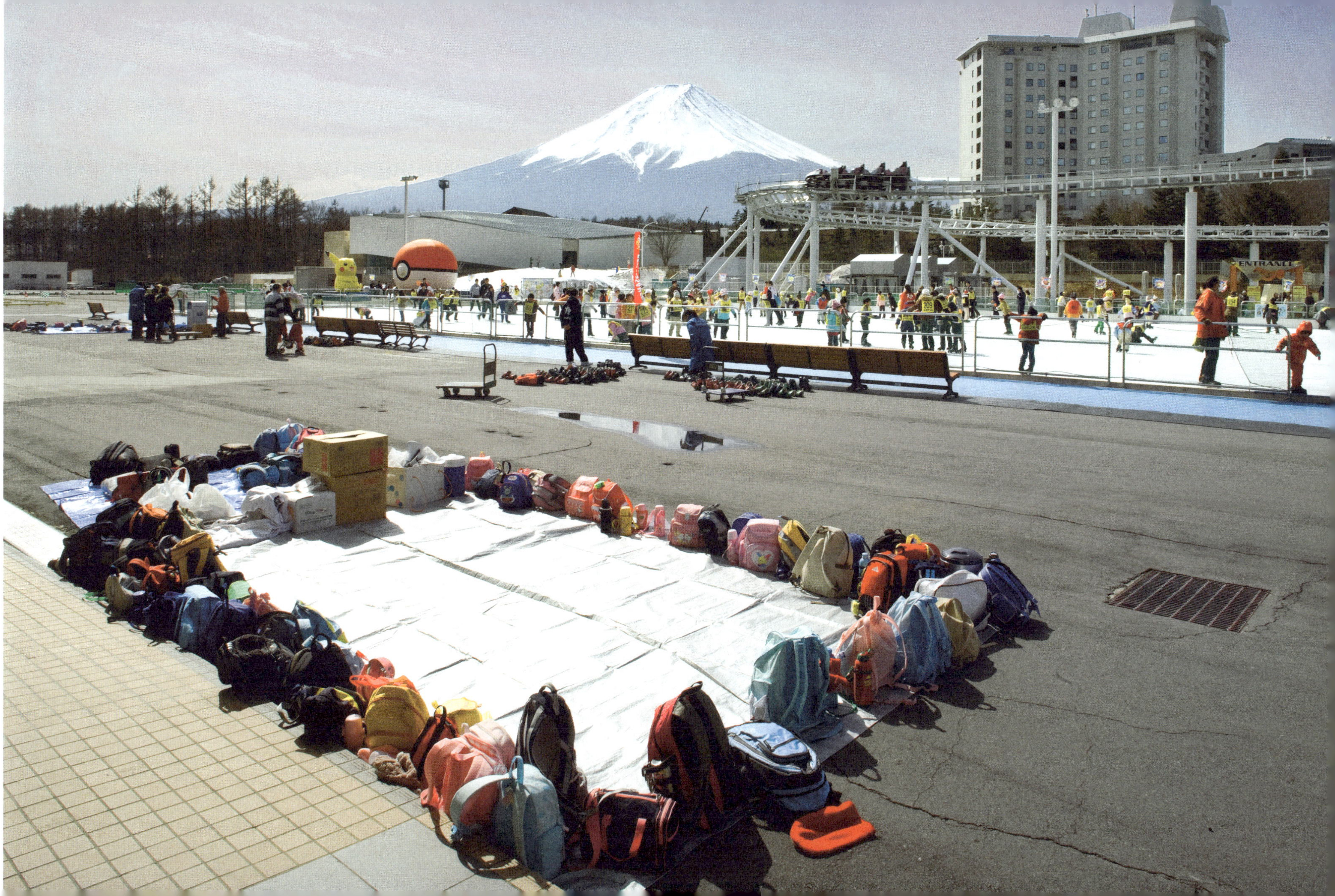
ENTRANCE

collective order | marius born

| 52

Dai-San, Daiba Historical Park, Tokyo, February 28, 4pm

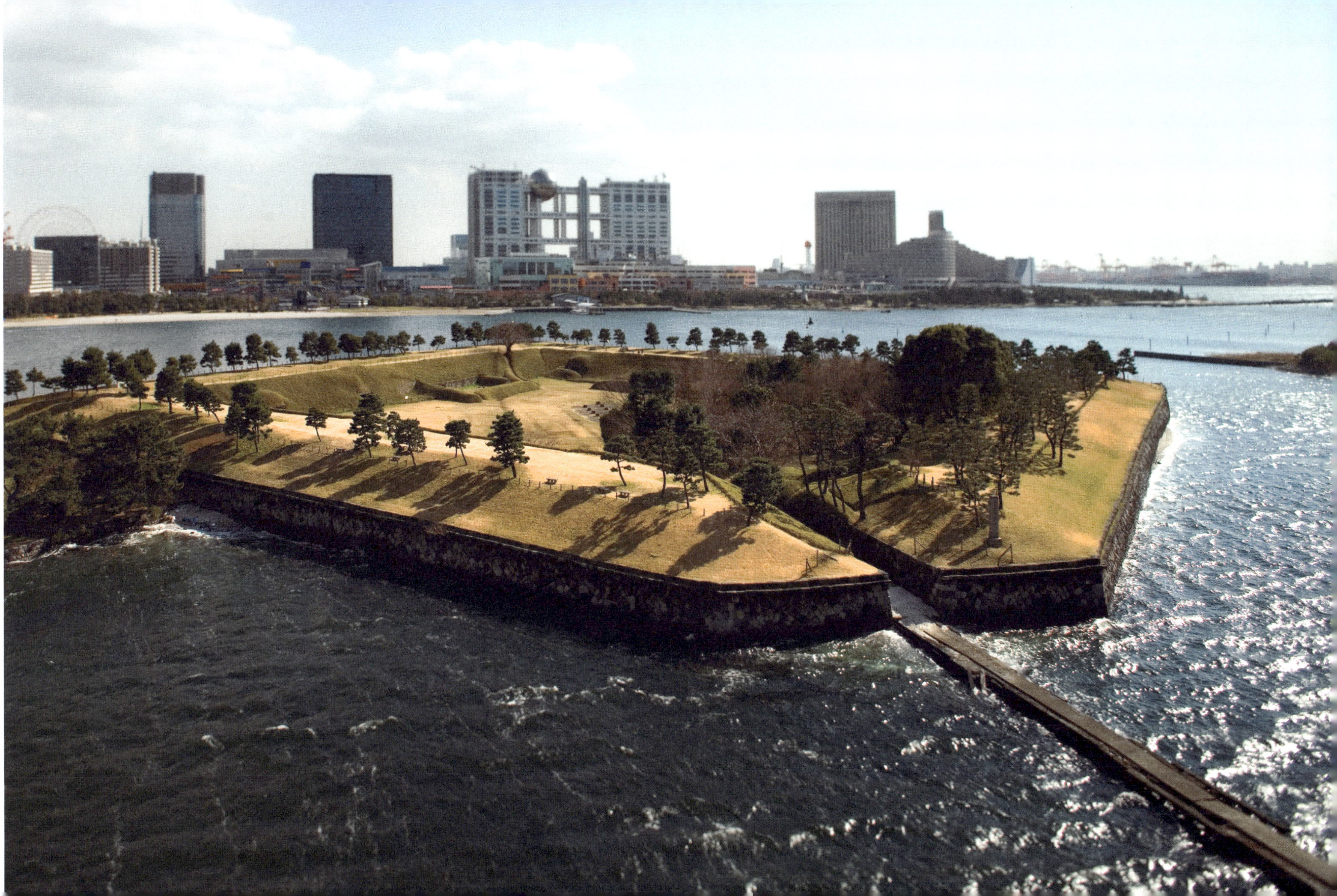

collective order | marius born

| 54

Nakayama Race Course near Tokyo, March 4, 3pm

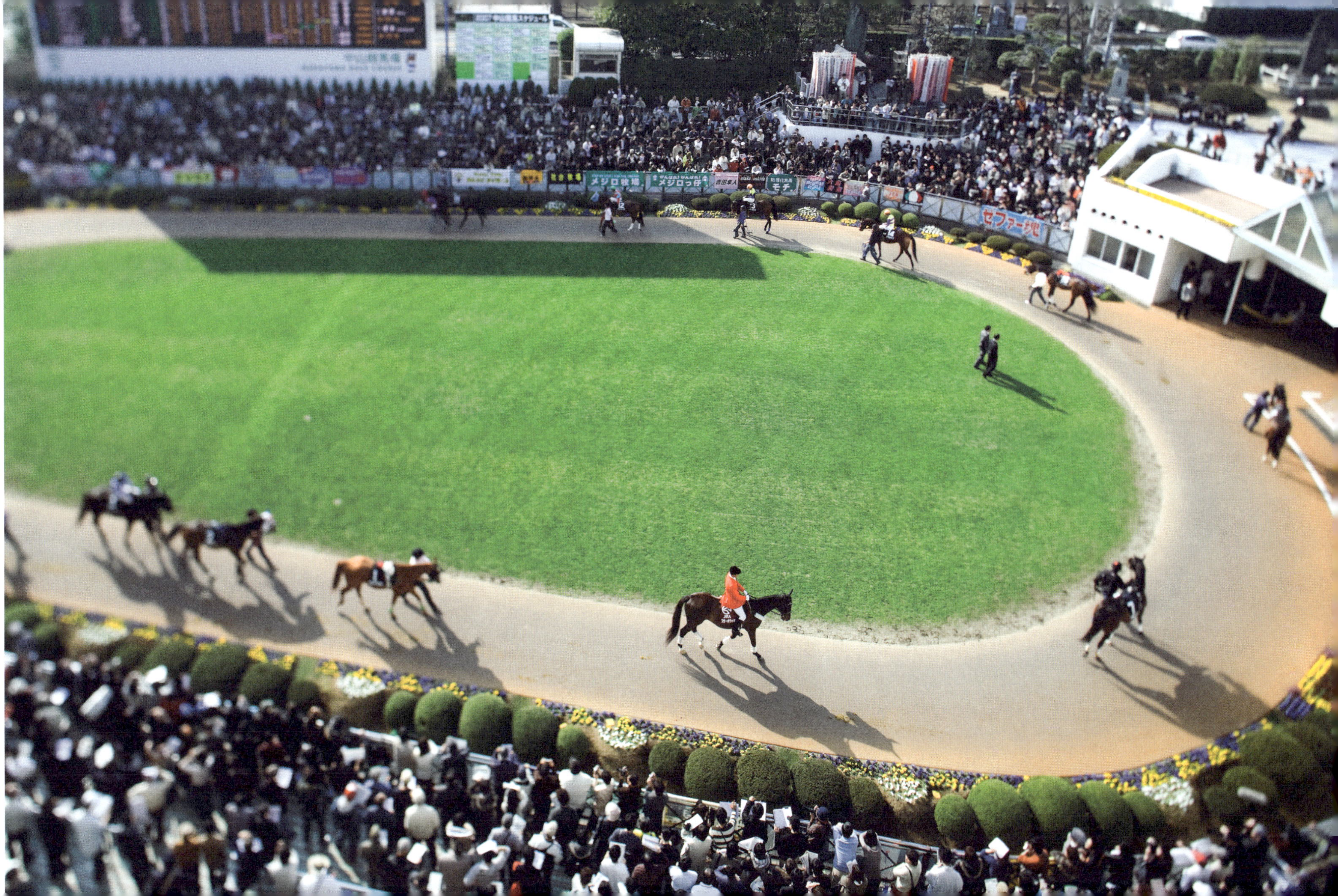

collective order | marius bom

| 56

Museum of Maritime Science, Tokyo, July 15, 3pm

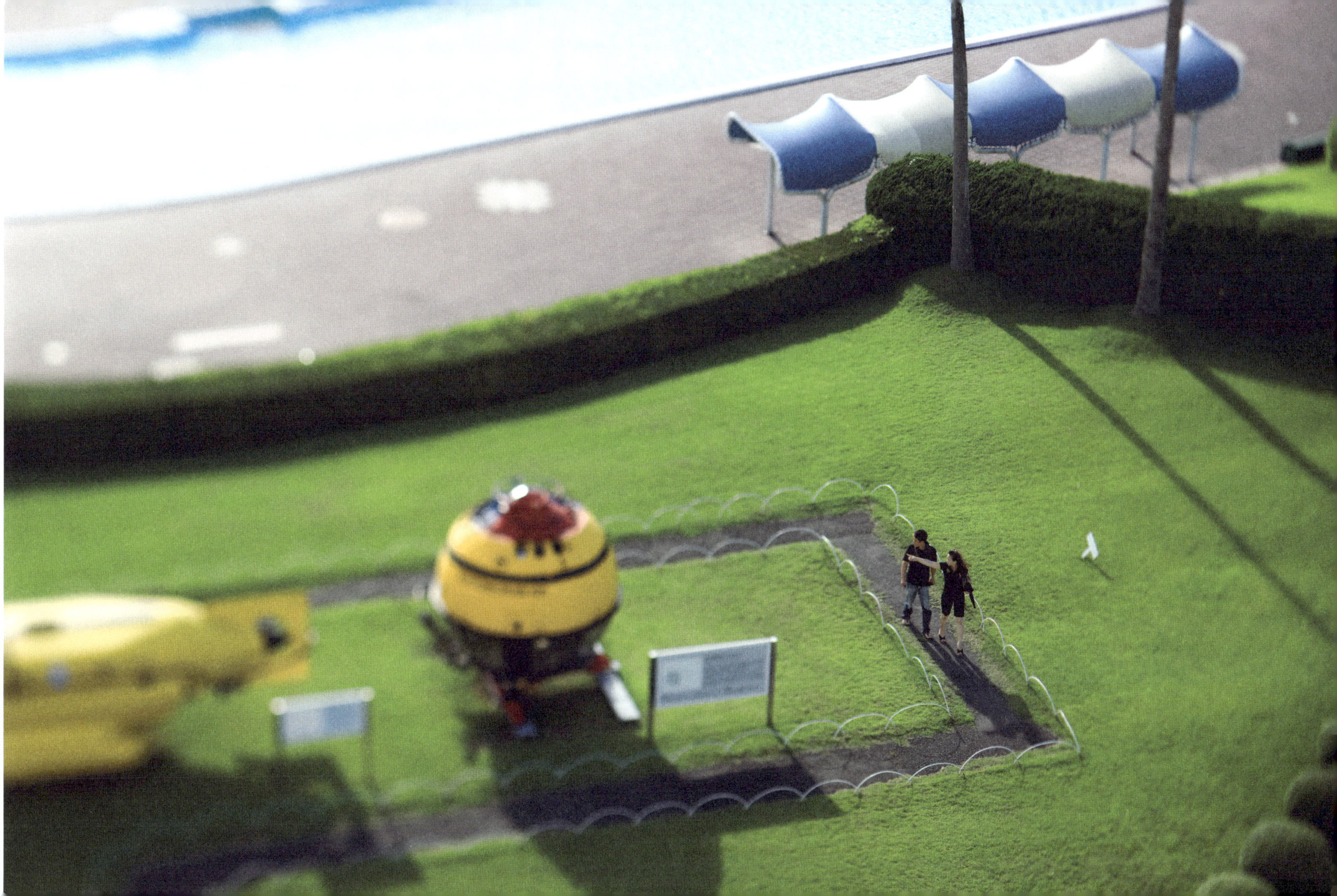

collective order | marius born

Museum of Maritime Science, Tokyo, July 15, 5pm

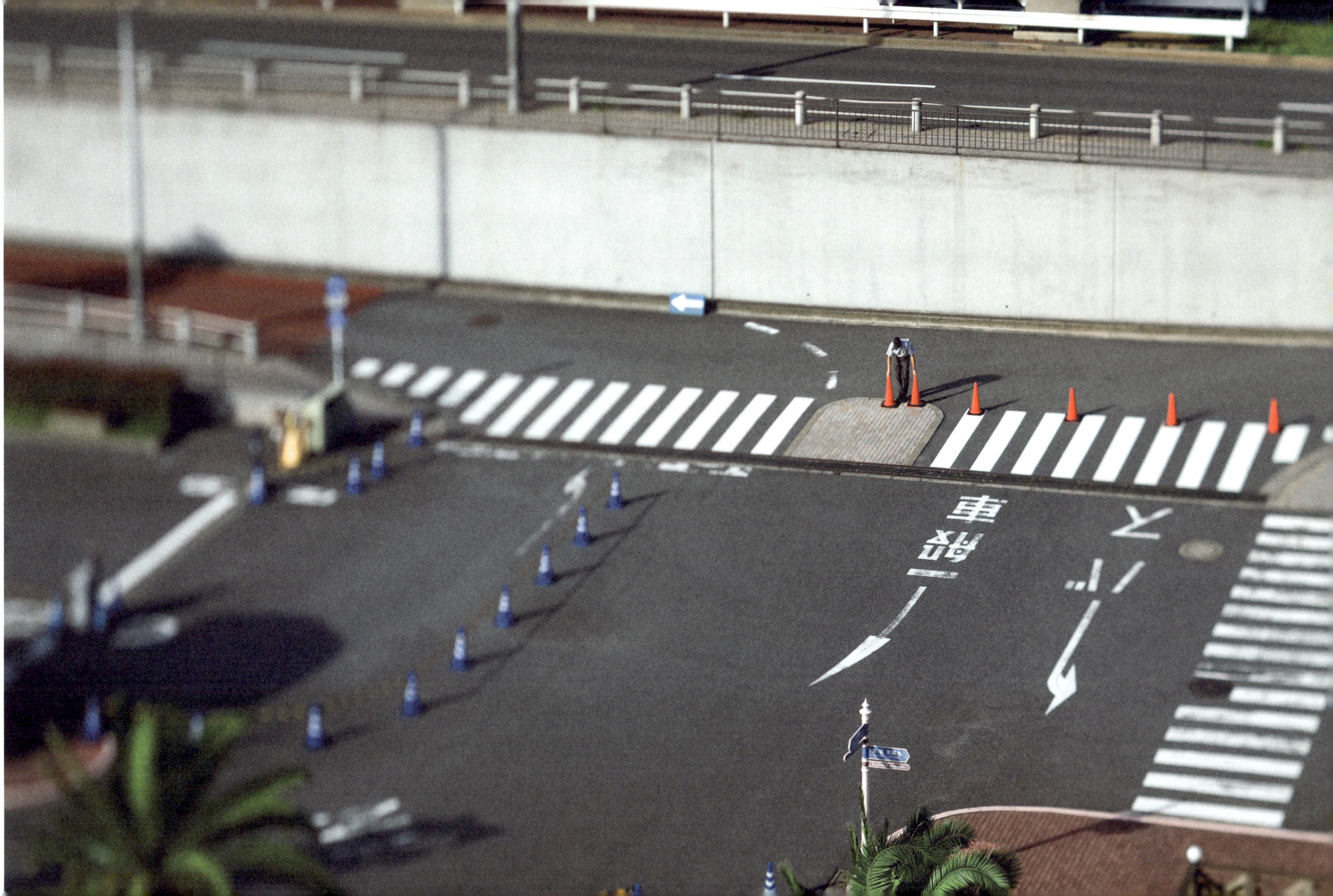

collective order | marius born

Fune-no-Kagakukan Station, Tokyo, July 15, 2pm

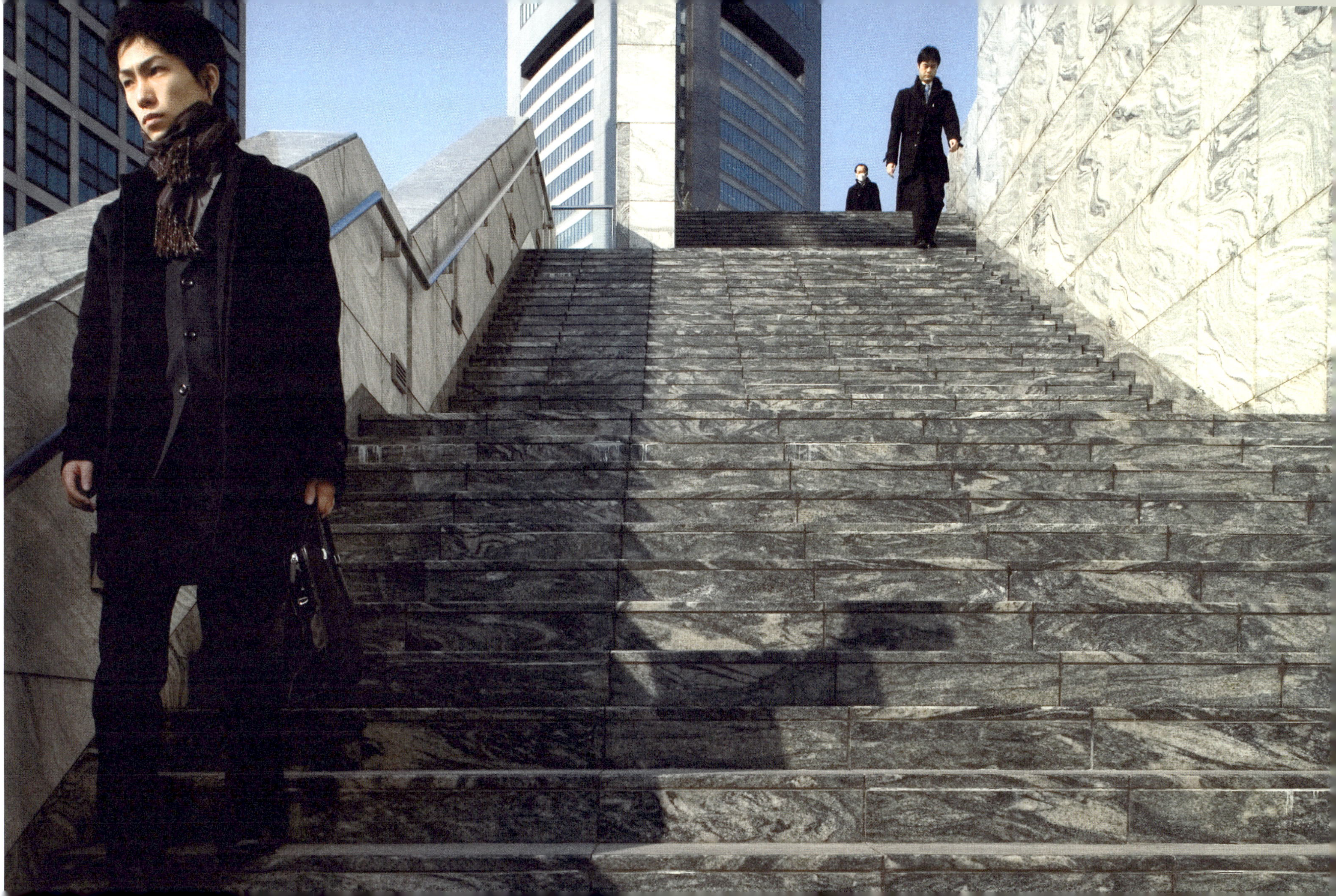

collective order | marius born

| 62

Toyosu, Tokyo, February 12, 1pm

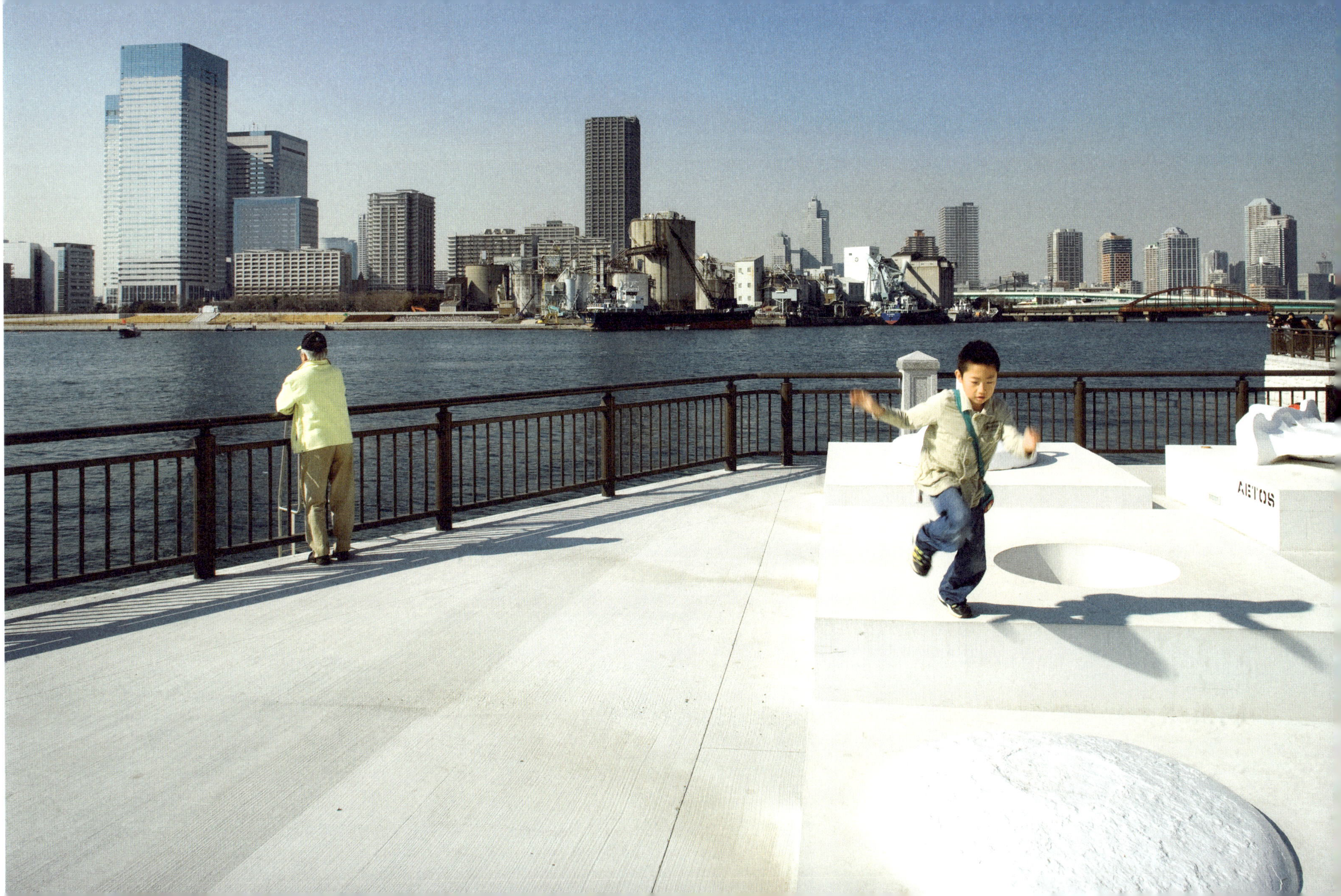
AETOS

collective order | marius born

| 64

Imperial Palace Plaza, Tokyo, March 9, 4pm

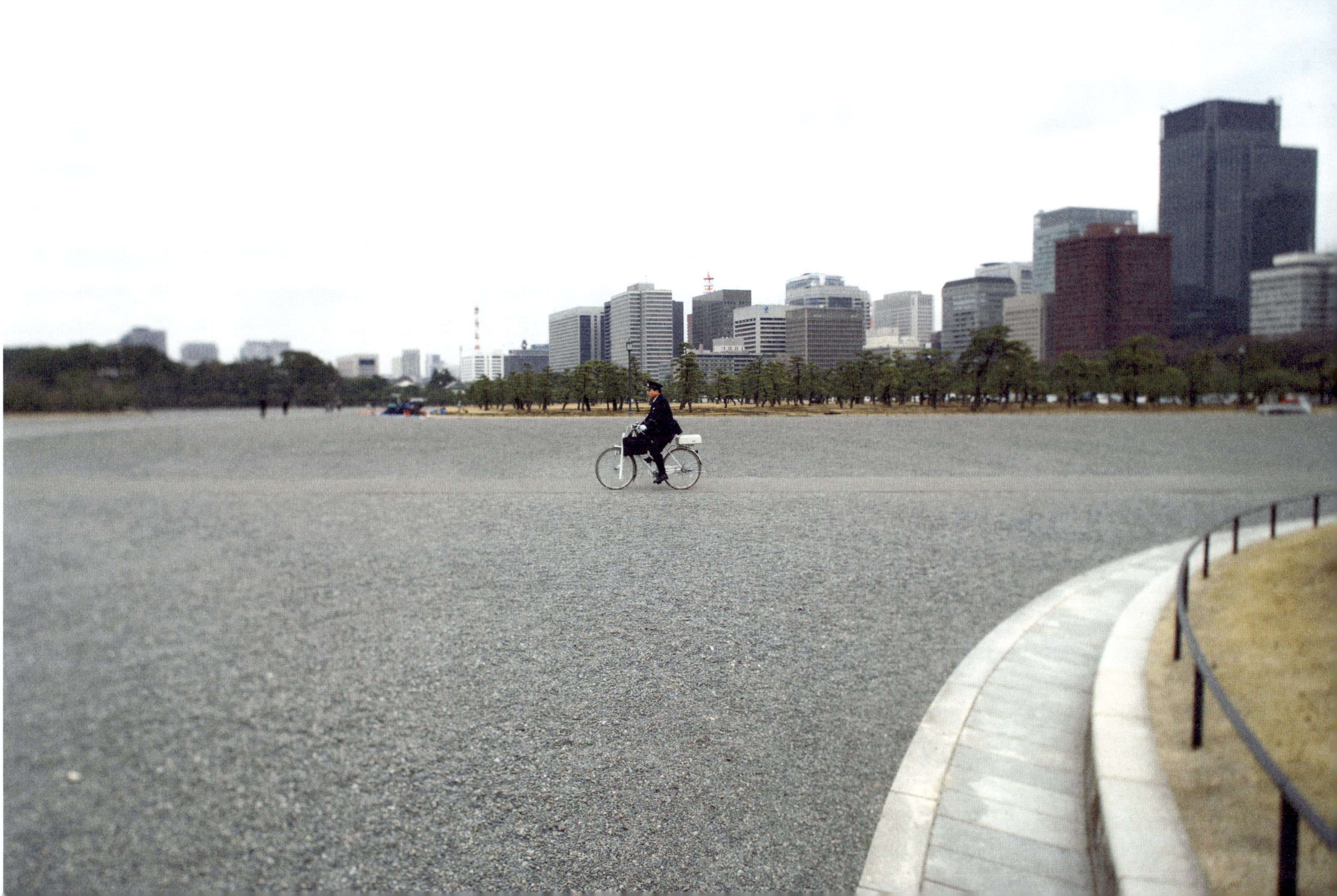

collective order | marius born

Roppongi Hills Tower, Tokyo, February 21, 1pm

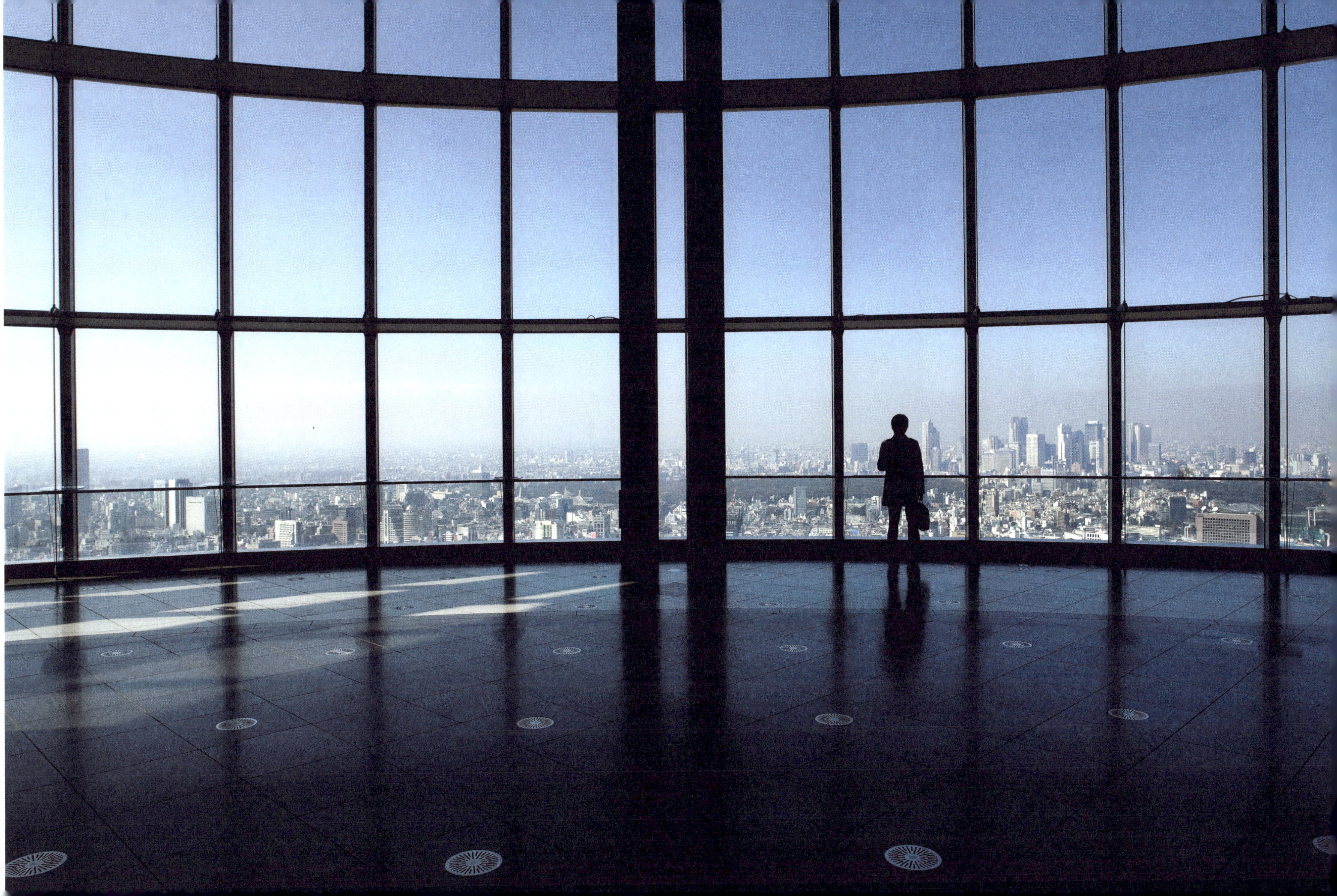

Tameike-Sanno Subway Station, Tokyo, March 8, 1am

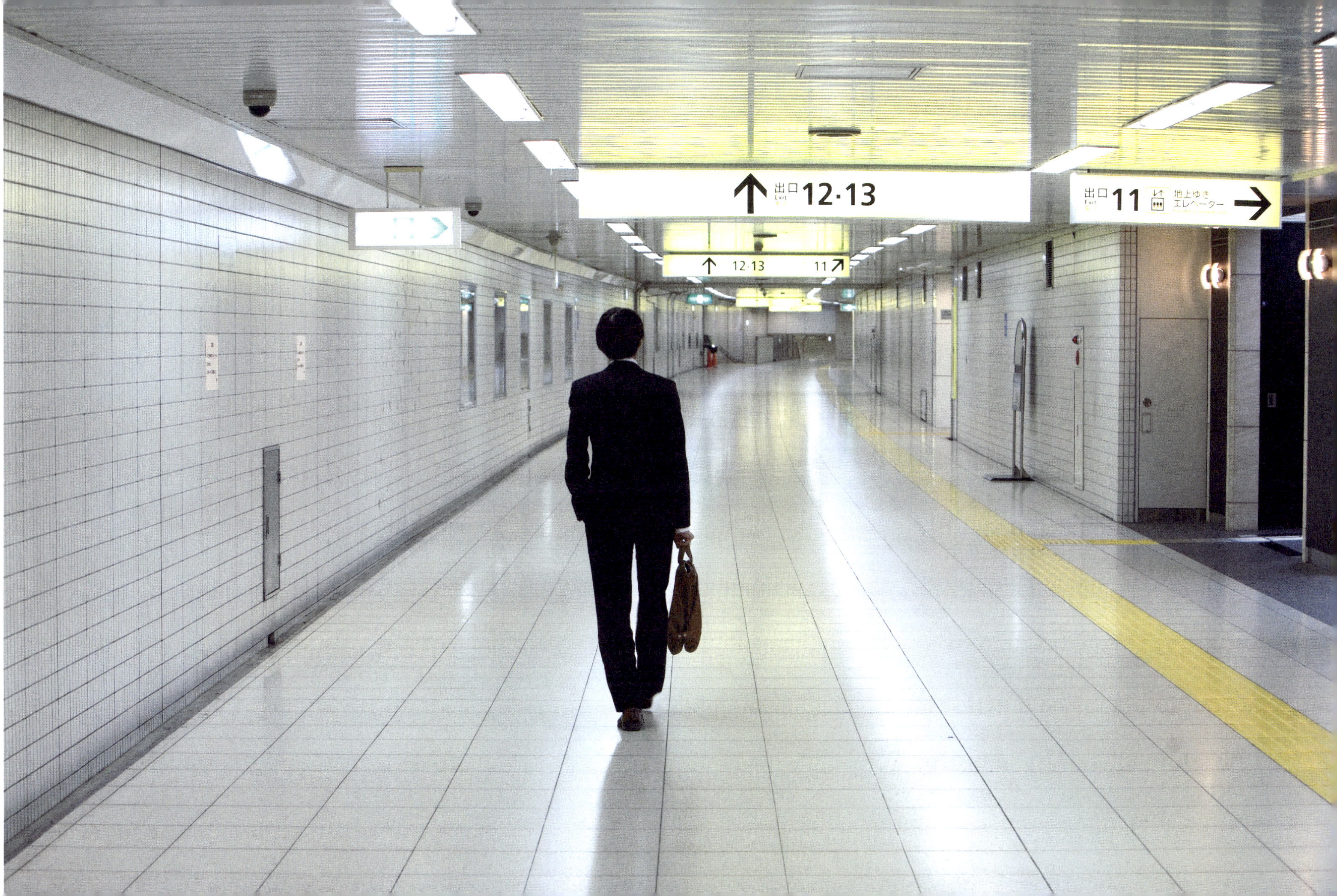
出口 Exit 12·13
出口 Exit 11
地上ゆき
エレベーター
12·13
11

© 2011 Marius Born, Marlies Whitehouse, Daniel Perrin and
Verlag der Buchhandlung Walther König, Köln

Design: Lilian-Esther Krauthammer, kussundbiss.ch
Lithogaphy: Peter Laely, panag.ch
Japanese translation: Yûichi Kitaguchi
Print: DZA Druckerei zu Altenburg

Published by Verlag der Buchhandlung Walther König, Köln
Ehrenstr. 4, 50672 Köln
Tel. +49 (0) 221 / 20 59 6-53
Fax +49 (0) 221 / 20 59 6-60
verlag@buchhandlung-walther-koenig.de

Bibliographic information published by the Deutsche
Nationalbibliothek
The Deutsche Nationalbibliothek lists this publication in the
Deutsche Nationalbibliografie; detailed bibliographic data
are available in the Internet at http://dnb.d-nb.de.

Printed in Germany

Distribution

Switzerland
AVA Verlagsauslieferungen AG
Centralweg 16
CH-8910 Affoltern a.A.
Tel. +41 (44) 762 42 60
Fax +41 (44) 762 42 10
verlagsservice@ava.ch

UK & Eire
Cornerhouse Publications
70 Oxford Street
GB-Manchester M1 5NH
Fon +44 (0) 161 200 15 03
Fax +44 (0) 161 200 15 04
publications@cornerhouse.org

Outside Europe
D.A.P. / Distributed Art Publishers, Inc.
155 6th Avenue, 2nd Floor
USA-New York, NY 10013
Fon +1 (0) 212 627 1999
Fax +1 (0) 212 627 9484
eleshowitz@dapinc.com

ISBN 978-3-86335-090-1

Special edition with a signed and numbered photo print
entitled "Tameike-Sanno Subway Station, Tokyo, March 6,
8.30am", published in an edition of 30 + 5 a.p. copies
in a presentation box (32 x 19.5 cm).

Cover:
Tameike-Sanno Subway Station, Tokyo, March 6, 8.30am

Back Cover:
Akihabara Electronic Town, Tokyo, February 15, 6pm

collective order | marius born | コレクティブ・オーダー

Marius Born | mariusborn.com
Born in 1969 in Zurich, Marius holds an M.A. in economics and business administration from the University of Zurich and a diploma in journalism from MAZ Lucerne.

His work for newspapers, non-profits and broadcast networks has taken him across the globe. Marius has received numerous awards and grants.

His reportage photography has been featured nationally and internationally. Marius is a visiting lecturer at the Zurich University of Applied Sciences, MAZ Lucerne and the University of St. Gallen.

Lieber Herr Imhoof

Weil kollektive Intelligenz nicht unbedingt eine Errungenschaft der Menschheit ist.

Herzlich Marius Born 19/08/13